The Bellfounder

☆

The Bellfounder
poems by Steven Toussaint

△

The
Cultural
Society

▽

Brooklyn MMXV

▽

The Bellfounder
ISBN 978-0-9887192-5-5
© 2015 by Steven Toussaint
all rights reserved

Contents

Eleanor,

"For you I have emptied the meaning / Leaving the song"

"Let us imagine for a moment that people have attained happiness—a state of complete human freedom of will in the widest sense: at that very instant personality is destroyed. Man becomes as solitary as Beelzebub. The connection between social beings is cut like the umbilical cord of a new-born infant. And consequently, society is destroyed. With the force of gravity removed, objects go flying off into space. (Of course some may say that society ought to be destroyed so that something completely new and just can be built on the debris! … I don't know, I am not a destroyer …)"

Andrey Tarkovsky, *Sculpting in Time*

The Bellfounder

The Ground

I embrace the bulk whole

as foregatherance
into cloud step, eddying, formative
but for deposits of cloud

abruption of cliff face sheer, downgrowth
commensurable with drought ends longing

as solstice parades
brilliantine by dredged embankments
brine seamed, milked at alpine view
is anyone there, is
anyone left
alive as white aster, as stars

hoove the ground
each order othering

to a bellows

I

Analogion

ore poured
through ode

and hissed forth
dread

child shape: O
caduceus floods

the log, reverse
osmosis of

cosmos through fog
so blunt, reluctant

the mind's
hand planting

shadows that HARK
swoons its likeness

through an icon's
drizzle field

as trident swayed
the ark, so lyre

slays the sun
exhaust spindrifts

toward a now
outmoded cloud

the same gasp
of late chimes

light snags
light once

absolved, now
cursed from form

outward
from cross-

beams of one word
embossed in the

thinning optic cup's
twice enameled

world, the worm's
realm is throat, all

thralldoms' germ
thou art, song womb

Cradle

(core)

miles beneath the drill

of an arbor   and still

    the blood hums   in sympathy

with the stiff

ascendancy of roots

      I voided

           what

     void *did*

sounded

    a flame's pronged vow

to become one

Organum

Listening for them.

As if disgorged
from keyboards

in the seabed,
scalloped

eyelids, black
'first matter'

thrusts fist
into fire.

Resounds
in the coarse

dross
hell churns out

at the edge of
boiling over.

<u>Early</u>

snow leaves

a circle

      beneath

  willow's bottle necklace

flower rubbed signs

deer shuffle by

              dark-

infused

as if

  long driven

Residuum

Objectless, yet
intense longing

sound bowed
at its thickest, split

branch over
fireproof ingots

of bronze.
The liquid, then

skimmed
of fragments,

lifted in drums
over pits

and carefully
tipped, so that

hot ore flowed
into space

between
two molds.

<u>Cradle</u>

(fissure)

as the sea eased into its glass

    hasp, into

        the belly

    of its wheel   the icons hatched

        in a flash of wing

        noiseless against

the fledged dark   that unstrummed

        fluttering

The Pond

like a portrait

in diptych, an
ebullient

screen, to
sip at

one's own mask

of nacre
is your silence

like that?
beneath

the cold reed

pads, a fish
shivers

dismailing

Twelfth

Night
ending
and

some
wind
and

dust
obscure
the

only
drunk
awake

who
can
hardly

see
the
peaks

from
the
bridge.

Conjunction

the so-called
'peacock's tail'

the ring of colors in the flask
subsides in time

making room for whiteness
the goddess Venus

even
over
mount-of-pines

the same up-
bubbling
that seized, once

a knuckle
of
clay from

the cavity-made-
shrine-
made-dwelling

had gradually
honey-
combed, had taken

by whatever
devilry
an opalescent

tinge, had
acquired a terrible
optics

air
coring
dust and

beasts
of the air
unheeded

except
by a stone's
silk nerves

and
somehow,
blacker than noon

shadow, horses
wade
through cold water

all
is vanity
and ashes, sings

mirror
from the baking
tunnel

all
these coils and
enclosures would

burst
into sand for, combust
and reflect

is fetish
in time's dreamy
depth amnesia, and upon

all
the soul's objects
an omni-

cidal glow, O
inward-
gazing, sings mirror

and under invisible
airborne
bodies

the day
goes
as the stream

or ridge
goes, all ways
oriented

toward some
un-
accounted-for

vortex, which is
the secret
of

all perfected
stances:
the birds fall, they

fail
identical
to lighting

above
the empty temple
O

a burning interval
poses
for

the adoration
of its
fugue-

body, a mono-
lith of repeating decimals
null-

set above
cross spars on which a body
burns

how
long is my root
mirror

sang, but wasn't
what heat!
what it meant to say

is a burning
body
faithful

to that
vocative
beam, seeming

a flare of all mouths
a burial
of time in hypnagogic

schist, in shale
where each
dream mutter

is a looking
glass, a song's re-
solve, sound-

proofed
to
inflection

coincidence, pre-
science, is
prophecy

is divine sequence
is ground, just
as quickly

taken
as given as
admonished

as one
might whip his apostle
O

hoards its
timepiece
somewhere

near
its ventilator, yet
this cockled-

glass-feeling
the air
has, means

it must be post-
matinal
and the creeping vine's

steady bounty
only
affirms

in apophatic re-
drafting, a
varnished sacrament

without half-
life
O

an absolute density
fed
back to itself

imbibes
its own manacled
twin, its

train of mists
its own libation, alms
straining late

survivor trees while
blight
overlords the duomo

the remnants
breathe
preempting

ripple, they test
mirror's
turgor

set fire
on
water

The Aleph

Golem
it's all possible

worlds I
give you not

giving you
words

the sigil-
wraiths, adepts

pretending at
Sibyl. Do you

remember
the flint prior

to light, the first
shrapnel?

Sublimity's
hidden leavings

all existent ice
melts down to?

All base metals
wish to be

good bells.

II

Measure

from pitch
back to its original

quiet tangle
of birchbark.

Down along
the frost encased

river, little
stinging reeds

thresh muscle
endlessly, stricken

to worry and ruffle
surfaces like this.

Enormous funnels
of pitch a people

press on, tamp
the thicket's

thickset quiet out
as if a current

of flame rouses
deep under boats

pitch-sealed
to carry them over.

Without an usher
or single familiar

landmark yet
the pilgrim

entering woods
hears pitch drip

from the sphere
of fixed stars.

Cradle

(moss)

dreamt in the white exclusive

    to mist

where chutes   patter strata

    of soft rock and

    loamy detritus

candleless, we're dipped

    shadows

in the plungepool's infusion

    of algae and

sunk creams

Imperium

grip the burning urn's lip naked
told I must arrive

naked here
in irradiant purses

the antique artillery basks
will you lead me further aflame?

Ur-Bell

I know
my absence

broods some
colossal

tongue
beating

angelus on
enormous

klaxons.

A scale
ascended, rung

smithing
rung.

The climb
is azure's

price or
pride

of Zion.

Idol breath
or wuther?

A flux-
addicted

susurrus, a

labyrinth
obsessed

that its
ends touch.

Blow my
mirror

if I be
conduit.

Nothing's too
scopic

to be prayed
at, body

full
of bowing.

Coin's quaver
at the center or

om's roar?
Call it

air.

An interned
but distant tin-

tin-
abulation

in the nether-
heaven.

The
neither/nor

of weather
suddenly

happening to
the foliate head

I remember.

I too was
pulled through

water to exalt
and turn, raying.

<u>Cradle</u>

(thicket)

nights   we slept in sheathes

      of earth, knees   tucked deep

in shadow, twinned

       where the veins pattern trees with

      shook light   where

the semblances   seeming   hasten

     the icons tear

Hubris

Asphyxed
alembic still

hawkwise,
cocksure.

Hear, Sphinx!
as the soul

to birdlime
goes in throes

it honks.

Dante's Ulysses

brothers of the
sunken star

Helian carved

sparest thereof
as Helen wept

opals, we share

a common
thread

we tread the
Orphic stair

though no cow-
eyed nymph

or goddess
follows there

in back of
orchard gates

she dances, dares
to break the apple

our trident-severed
vessel

we were spared

to make of our
tongues, our supper

our words
are congruent flares

appropriated
passions purge

all warmth we
could have nursed

or knelt

in the midst of
look

I work with sticks
in the dark

to ward off
consummation

witness tasks
atonement, so

in blows
warmer bass

intoned below
the bow

the pounce attempts
to parrot

while bats

pass over, numb
with murk

I heard
myself, my face

descried
in ruins

resolving tones
behind a congress

of tongue
and gums

I'll leave off

before
the lowing starts

I know enough

of surface
but depth

is insatiable
and so I swerve

from the
shadowless dirt

Cradle

(gorge)

moving? you'd risk   as if leprous, sifted clean

                              through your own ignominious

     flesh, a bog-   clogged flume   but savage in motion

                    this river

like a dawn-struck sword   in constant chasming

              its likeness   to wing bone, to gilded

                              carriage, any self-forgetting   chiasmus

                         only symptom

of a deeper stirring   a further dark

     blanket, under

          statement   *stream?*

Having been permitted

to wander
the ante-
pasture

lately bare
of
foxglove's

pretext
snow

gnawed down
to ascetic

thirst, I scan

the stillness here
for a certain defect

on the surface
a procession

of children
might have left

that their games
be counted
in memory

despite
having been
on all sides

flanked by ice
until

what's empty
no longer
serves

discipline but

calves a wailing
multitude:

words

not-made-
by-hands

won't touch
what hands

cannot

not knowing
their own
print yet, how

ice is known

to give way
by the arrival

of hallowed
grasses

<u>After</u>

words, to

ward

the parts

inside us we

cannot see

alive

III

In the middle of the journey

I came to myself
reading

some matter of saturnine greens

how, earthbound, bearing almseed
the winged rod overshot
its metallurgic root

between a spotted beast and home

let me bring to belling
in ouroboric air

why the stone is animal like our blood

The Work

that we may do   in words

      as she doth in as many years

dissolve   ascending

           by the dry way

     in a flask

   in a sand bath

           by the wet way

in a water bath, descend

self-fed   glass

      subtiliates

          in cold hands

      stridulates

          in phials

in circulating vessels

      pelicans and double pelicans

Newtonian ova rinsed in the metaline depths

earthenware box   made only of earth

    wherein atoms urge, fizz

        bevel   fulge into light

ash couples in surf

        the sea   a-box-containing-other-boxes

    sand bathes

    the muddled ferns

Melismata

of light
rain, light

in abundance

but small.
Flattened

at the base of

two
mountains'

timely
collision

the base
of me now

cobalt
leaf also

amalgam
of plague

and fragrance
I prayed for

each hand's
burning

branch
that sputter

of blood breath
and water.

Cradle

(aerie)

among limbed winds

burned huge

        effigies, bundles

of dirge

    our drudge

this counting, this

remoteness in dust, once

     fledged

it leaves this smokeprint

     sheds its surface leading up

Silentium

polygonal
moss over

flowing
monuments

each one
degenerates

approaches
apeirogon

Chrysopoeia

Ichorous tissue
cooling nude

on the bone
in this sieve

we achieve
transparency

reading fluent
from news

and weather a
sudden rose's

snaked-off skin
the glass apple

a crushed
and humble light

onyx preserves
makes possible

whose core is
ark air.

Plainsong

not
two
it
is

one
the
ear
the

heart
the
air
the

breath
starts
one
hearth

one
hand
on
earth

The Bell Player

peering over
his ropes

and casement
which tow

the voices
up, we are

wordless
ourselves, faces

who blink
in his song

strand us
on high alps

strangers
to those who

live below
the tarns

the stones
which replace

our hearts
crossed a great

expanse once

Cradle

(rose)

in a contrail

      glyph

in a bounding particle, all flesh

its pleated crystals

       chew, in vowels carries me drowsy

bellowed

   each

   O, a

little   G-d

Alms

from
green sheaths

gold-

pistoled
spires
herald

pike-shaped cells

solar imbued

itinerant
moons

their self-

similar cursive
writ circum-
gyre

in tidal pools

an insular
elliptic

iterating

sea rose or
diaphanous

as bridal quarter
curtains are

as empyreal lips
part

yielding
organ tones

ballasted

to undules
of blessing

in tendril time

the music
itself

un-
scored
growth

Dawn Chorus

people

won't be

people, people

won't be

people, weeping

Tabula Rasa

starts

a numeral's
seed

a decimal slit at
star's edge, held

on the tongue
like a razor

like the scroll
of sting, inside

who jump-
starts its own

heart manually
thralling

the sequence
through its

lone
quartz eye

feed-
back de-

tached
a mass-

less roar
a maze un-

furled
its golden

mean, en-
rapt

somewhere
the words

for
words are

lost wax, casting
labyrinth debris

into a half-

step, the
gold rooting

in grids
of cream

in words

the words
herded, hours

chorded

in the brood-
comb's drone

the light
already coming

in retches
we're watching

a winged
effigy's

helixed
vanishing

the notch acquiring
nerves, lashes

shadow pours
its ores

into
the breath-

upended
spire, its

gyred
inner fuses

funneling
Os down

to single
macula, point

at which the
static-flushed

voice of monks
touched

the prism's
bottom-

less spine

the mind
inside its

thrashed
alb

where the
halves spread

their black
fins

the blind voice
bulbs

blip
of

some
lamp

sapling
curls

in
dark

arterial
silk

Notes

"Passio" adopts a line and a number of figures from Andrey Tarkovsky's film, *Andrey Rublyov* (1966).

"Dante's Ulysses" is a reimagining of *Inferno* XXVI. "Having been permitted" revisits Robert Duncan's meadow, now a frozen and liminal space.

A number of lines in "The Work" were adapted from Athanasius Kircher's alchemical treatise, the *Mundus subterraneus* (1665). I consulted many Renaissance alchemical texts during the writing of *The Bellfounder*, and figures from these texts precipitate into the poems. I am especially indebted to the *Chymicall Treatise* of Arnoldus de Nova Villa (1611), which furnished the final line of "In the middle of the journey," and Elias Ashmole's *Way to Bliss: In Three Books* (1658).

"Plainsong" arpeggiates a chord by Ronald Johnson ("BEAM 24").

"Tabula Rasa" presents a close listening to the orchestral work of the same title by Arvo Pärt (Ulster Orchestra, 1999).

Acknowledgments

Thank you to the editors of the following publications for giving many of these poems a first home: *Conjunctions, Court Green, The Cultural Society, ika, Letters, LVNG, OmniVerse, Occasional Religion, Shearsman,* and *TYPO.*

I want to thank especially Zach Barocas for your support and your Society.

I have been blessed with teachers. Thank you Joshua Marie Wilkinson, Cole Swensen, Geoffrey G. O'Brien, Elizabeth Robinson, and Rod Smith. I have been blessed with friends, brilliant and bewildering. Thank you to my Iowa family, especially Nicholas Gulig, Ally Harris, and Jane Wong. You shared your poems with me. I hope to become worthy of that immense generosity.

To my family, thank you. I love you.

The Bellfounder benefitted from careful readers early on. Thank you Elizabeth Robinson, Lee Posna, and Max Porter. And special thanks to Peter O'Leary for the best lunch of my life.

Finally, thank you Eleanor Catton, beloved.

Steven Toussaint was born in Chicago in 1986. He is the author of the chapbook *Fiddlehead* (Compound Press, 2014). He lives on the side of a volcano in Auckland, New Zealand.

△ △ ▽ ▽

The Bellfounder
was printed in an edition of 250 copies
on Glatfelter 55# Natural Offset Antique
by McNaughton & Gunn

Text was set in Adobe Jenson Pro, Avenir, and Kaffi

Design by Jon Grizzle
Photograph by Timothy Nazzaro